I Should Never Have Fired the Sentinel

Jennifer LoveGrove

I Should Never Have Fired the Sentinel

Jennifer LoveGrove

ECW PRESS

MISFIT

Published by ECW PRESS
2120 Queen Street East, Suite 200, Toronto, Ontario, Canada M4E 1E2

LIBRARY AND ARCHIVES CANADA CATALOGUING IN PUBLICATION

LoveGrove, Jennifer
I should never have fired the sentinel / Jennifer LoveGrove.

"A MisFit book."
Poems

ISBN 1-55022-670-3

I. Title.

PS8573.O875412 2005   C811'.6   C2004-907056-8

Editor for the press: Michael Holmes
Cover and Text Design: Darren Holmes
Cover Image: Sandra Alland in collaboration with Corrina Hodgson
Author Image: Sandra Alland
Typesetting: Mary Bowness
Printing: Gauvin Press

This book is set in AGaramond and Futura

The publication of *I Should Never Have Fired the Sentinel* has been generously
supported by the Canada Council, the Ontario Arts Council, and the Government of
Canada through the Book Publishing Industry Development Program. Canada

DISTRIBUTION
CANADA: Jaguar Book Group, 100 Armstrong Ave., Georgetown, ON L7G 5S4

PRINTED AND BOUND IN CANADA

ECW PRESS
ecwpress.com

Table of Contents

Fully Autonomous Planets

The Right Defence

I am touched by your little gift
of lies, how you built
them out of love,
how there was nothing else to do.

— Libby Scheier

And, Go!

When the whistle keens, I crawl back inside the CAT scan machine —
itself a form of lechery. Where is the lost and found here?
A slow leak, a squandering, the economics
of *this way that way without pausing endless endless* —

No. Everyone knows you can't shove a hurricane
back into the jar it came from. Not even you.
I should never have fired the sentinel. He was
doing a fine job, and now look at the mess

the lawn is in. Apple cores, arms, those little hairs
I loved when they were still on your knuckles.
You can't live on Novocaine alone. Not any more.
I change my mind, I don't want to be

disinterred. Someone should apologize
to all those orphaned shoulders.
It is the National Croquet Tournament
of Regret. You can sign up here.

The Lifeboat

We live on a fat red lifeboat,
heaving and tossing
on a geyser of melted gold
siphoned from the veins of the dead.

A pox of small explosions
tears up the rubber
beneath our feet.
If you squint,
you can even see it
from the moon.

Some of us fall over the sides
but do not splash. The rest
are charming enough,
with those little crossbows,
but confused by all these
lights and noises!

Those who still have legs
try to jump —
as the fiery dots
connect themselves,
hungry as barrels.

Long-term Effects

This air is antiseptic and I slide out,
leaving my slippers behind. I am stealthy,
secrets hidden like credit cards in my shoe.
Hop the tracks and walk tightrope over the dark ravine.

There are women everywhere:
women in boxes, women in walls,
women in trees and dirt, in elevators
and hand-cranked, levitating beds.

I build joists from everything
on this street: broken drawers, lilacs, wet needles
and offers of credit repair. These will stretch
through fear — a solid, level floor.

Helen Clark's Garrison

for Marsden, after one week

You are not interested in subterfuge
or tax evasion, or even our most recent
defensive drills. You squint through
bleary eyes, then sleep it off. I don't
blame you one bit. The nap widens

into dreams, spectres of warriors —
each face a maze of ink and pride.
Do not cry yet, it will grow
more complicated; just ask the woman

who runs the country you smuggled
yourself into. You're doing a fine job!
She may promote you next month:
to keepsake, or Chief Sommelier;
to harbinger, or even mastodon.
There may be some

commuting involved, but you are
nearer the south pole than I.
You are nearer the moon, in fact —
could you speak up, when
the time comes?

Piñata

There is always one
at the party who strikes
a little too hard, both hands
and a snarl. The other guests
can see your teeth, wet
and bristling. At first they laugh
and miss their turn. Then
look at one another,
take a step back.

They cover their children's eyes —
this is not television. They can
hear you heave and grunt, the game
careens, then splinters. Someone
coughs, you are trying
to catch your breath.

The yard is a groundswell
of treasure and awkwardness.
You keep the blindfold
on, used to cold drafts
and intuition. You know
you can't just crack
something open
and pick out the good bits.

Bulldozer

Lately, my sleep is landfill.
Pockmarked with plastic bags
that hold a fondness for rupture,
politically motivated erosion
and dinner party small talk.

I blink the guests into strangers
who whisper words like "bulldozer"
into designer cufflinks.

Last weekend, a neighbour siphoned
the brake fluid for cocktails.
In celebration, it zoomed down the hill,
razed the ambassador's fence,
Benz, wife.

Now the government monitors
the site, edges around my bed.
If I close both eyes, everything
will rot; there will be
picketers with signs:
"Regrets only."

Dear Recidivism

I wish to de-enrol from your class.
I can't see the board over the phallus
looming above the desk
in front of me anyway.

What is that tremolo
gurgling around
our pinstripe rows? Once
I would have said "rats"
but I know better — I know
what "relocation" means.
It doesn't mean clean.
It means your chin juts
at an angle you call jaunty.

Still, you are a lousy facilitator.
No chairs for our sore backs —
you expect us to lean,
hover, topple.

Where do I reclaim my vertigo?
They made me check it at the gate
with my "unmentionables,"
like foresight and fingernails.

All I did is have hands!
Blame me, blame me not.
I would never recognize
a truant officer,
even if I still had eyes.

Yessir, sincerely, Yessir.

Immunization

A virus can galvanize in copper
or that which tastes of copper.
Patterns of ones and zeros —
mosquitoes in pairs, a funnel cloud.

We recoil, despite the netting — one of many
barricades. Grip the arms of our deck chairs.
By noon, gave up fighting indoors,
thought the air would disperse

accusations, blame, reprisals. A pinch
and I kill instantly. A streak of blood
determined to stretch
all the way to ragged elbow. Too late.

I have been drained, and still so much
further to go. The only way to drink
quinine is with sugar, but you trust nothing
I offer. All of today is contagion.

The Right Defence

> ". . . this winter holds in it all winters past,
> back to those of the elders who wrote
> that our way is marked out,
> that we already belong to Love or to Fire."
> — Jorge Luis Borges, "Cambridge"

A bipolar cold has glazed the months. I learn real joy
and real panic. Reflections in metal, and in ice.
That acknowledging the impossible will
never resolve it. That it was only impossible
when you named it so.

Your left palm opens to a single sequin.
A plaintive offering, meant fondly. We are both
blinded, at least, for a season. Who is the thief,
and who is the fence?

You hand me the gas can, give me over to Fire,
then charge me with danger. Solid defence can get you
out of third degree burns, and I am deft at dodging blame.

There is a truth in recklessness, but also
walls and fractures. All danger is glamour,
and all glamour is illusion. I have resealed
the sound barrier. I bring you back
a souvenir — a pocketful of ash.

When they finally come for us, rattling
chains and simple equations, all your charges
will be dropped. They will find me on the ice —

crossing over, crossing over, crossing over.

Waivers

Look up: a mania of blue,
nothing is falling. Intact is
intact. The latest referendum:
whether or not
to ossify the sky. You know,

protect ourselves from the stick men
up there on the scaffold, their quivering
and restless crossbows angled
always toward our kneecaps.

The haberdasher of foresight
has resigned, escorted himself out
of our periphery. Another boarded up
exponent: here comes the Starbucks,
the Chicken Little Clause, the waivers
we've put the world on.

The Invitation

An invisible hand punches a hole into blue
over Lake Huron. Glowing pink keyhole
dares us to enter another sky — neon, thick,
seeping out like panic. We paddle toward the gap,
we'll sneak through. No matter our burning arms
or the shadows of those on shore
shouting warnings at our wake.
This time we'll make it.

And the ones on the other side?
Living perpetually in fuchsia ooze, dragging
their seven arms, like oars, through quicksand air.
They wade into sparse, economical blue,
shoving pink aside like a protesting mob. I've yet
to catch sight of one of them — renegade or lost child —
bursting through, triumphant, the day no longer resisting
their soupy attempts at velocity.

Instead, pink winks out — again we miss
the brief invitation. White dots poke through,
my arms prickle, and I take your hand,
one of two.

Scarecrows

She says people are mostly
made of helium.
No red spatters, nothing
dense as calcium,
integrity, inertia.

They fly off when she glances away,
strings writhing cloud-bound —
all her friendships, a discredit to gravity.

She is more careful now, experiments
with knot-work — nylon, twine,
piano wire. Now a fixation with dirt,

planting, food. A garden of heavier anchors:
carrots, rutabagas, yams.

Her station wagon in neutral,
engorged with bricks —

our arms rise up
against the windows.

Shred

May stretches before us, flat,
a desert, and Prom Night sits up
bright as Vegas. We will ride in
on camels, in limos, rattle dice
like snakes, sixes every time.

No. Glamour and I are bankrupt,
spent, flat on our backs, feet
holding up what air still hangs above us.
I shred my cuticles like documents.
Hacksaws of fingernails — I scrape
and tear and, always, I am surprised
by the blood. It seeps; a rumour,
a broken yolk. This is high school.

We give up rolling our eyes, stab
tickets to bulletin boards
next to the heads of Siouxsie Sioux
and Tracy Tracy. We sneer
at the preps, the jocks, all fuchsia
taffeta and matching cummerbunds —
molluscs boiled in cough syrup.

We claim our own opulence:
steal our kid brother's favourite
marble, slam it through
an empty bottle, a precise spin
and crack against a Doc sole.
Gore the air with a Players Light,
suck and hack, lungs
full of storm clouds.
It will be years before
we can roll proper joints, years
before we stop choking.

*   *   *

Zach waves a walking stick
like a wand. He Sinatras the hall
in a top hat and shorts,
red Converse and a bow tie.
I kiss him full on the lips,
hot for the sorcery of it all.

We lean against a monotony
of lockers, punch-dented metal
along the science lab. We hate
Mr. Raddick the most, he sputters
freaks and *faggots*, suggests we try
drunk driving. We contaminate
the Honour Roll. A Boy Scout badge
for *Redneck*, left like an apple on his desk.

Zach slips me the tongue,
intent and probing, a hungry eel.
My boyfriend's gulping JD
in the boys' room, thinks
he's a bad ass. I hate
his silver suit, jacket slashed
to the waist, his armour,
the cold blade sparring
of our talk. He refuses
to sleep with me. It is worse
than cheating.

*   *   *

This shit's good, Zach says,
plants a small white square
beneath my tongue. *Not like that*
strychnine shit the skids sold us.
Two days to unravel myself,
muscles cramped in voodoo knots,
whiplash panic, and the same
maudlin Michael Stipe 'til dawn.
Zach leans back, winks assurance:
I got this from Donnie.

Donnie's a real punk — green 'hawk
and 20-holes, carved his credibility
into his forearm, double fisting
a guitar string and a Bic pen.
His acid splits open
the night, Zach's walking stick pulls
falling stars to the floor.

The walls bend and lunge,
dissolve in ripples, my arms
whirl comet-tails around my head,
a halo, a helicopter. I soar through a clutch
of hyenas, dresses, cheerleaders,
by my boyfriend, arms like boas
around my best friend. "Stairway to Heaven."

A tree waits across the street
and I climb, shoes tossed down like scabs.
My dress snags but I am beyond fashion,
beyond gravity, perched in a cotton
candy tree. Shouts gouge the trunk, leaves
rattle and others stumble.
Zach loses his cane, a car revs, a cheap hotel
swallows us whole.

I tell no one I'm a virgin. Fake
that I've done it, *Breakfast Club*
bravado. Lions' Park, Kinsmen Park,
the back seat of my dad's Impala.

Sure it hurts at first —
I smirk — *but it's worth it.*
They sway in, cupped for more,
but I am coy. *Find out*
for yourselves, already.

X-Ray

Night slides its film of dread
between your jaws, a flash of light
and everyone can see you flinch.

Morning shoulders your chest.
Predictable, but even less welcome
than the day before —
a pried open ribcage.

The Argument

You see those rows of faces
bobbing in the grandstand?
It is you they are laughing at.
How you dress up your laziness
in corsets and military garb,
manufacturing drills and indecipherable schedules.

Onstage, you know everyone's lines
but your own. You've mastered the rhetoric
of productivity. All the mirrors smile
and shake your hand.
Untie the blindfold, turn
around, take a bow.

I will not let you out of the basement
to help untie anything.
All your glistening machines
are under review. You shake the hand
of tyranny, swell pink and round for days
after he compliments your grip.

All the meetings are convening
with your chair empty. No one notices.
If you are cold
there are some matches in the tin.
Your best suit will flare up nicely.
Don't forget to eat the apple
I left in the pocket.

Lost Kids

She is four, her dad's granite hand hauls her
to Canadian Tire. Rows of drill bits, screwdrivers, hockey sticks
do not pull her in like magnets. Adrift in muttering,
he turns small machines over in his hands.
She slides away to the toys.

Dolls and horses in boxes — faces beam behind plastic windows,
begging to play, needing haircuts and magic marker tattoos,
craft scissor amputations. She smiles and the floor heaves —
the aisle yawns into a long hallway, a medieval chill.
Toys dissolve in the cold around her.

The hall dead-ends. Iron doors slam —
steel ring handles, unblinking eyes. The walls sway,
lined with thousands of pairs of blue jeans
slumped over hangers — resolute, tidy.

She can't find her dad, her voice hides under her tongue.
Feet too are mutinous, march her deeper.
A cold wind shoves her
toward the doors.

Wakeful parents hear screaming,
try untangling her from sweat-drenched sheets.
She hurtles past racks of jeans —
a cold salt pours, and she knows:
every hanging pair

used to be a lost kid. Punished
for wanting toys that factory work can't afford,
for wandering alone, for pocketing gum
at checkout — they all end here, never worn,
immobile — perfect.

This knowledge releases the locks,
the doors swing open, and there — reigning, hovering,
legs wide in command, hands on hips
if he had hands — is the biggest pair of jeans
she's ever seen.

He sprints down the hall and she runs.
Rather, concentrates hard on the idea
of running. Cast in stone, her feet
anchor her, as he sprints fast through air.

Already turning blue, she crawls
along the flytrap floor — not fast enough —
toward the row of blond cashiers. They smile,
waving their arms like frantic antennae.

Attention: Recidivism

You are winning. These pills
do not close my eyes. Planets
without names nudge
the periphery. She should never
have skipped school.

I ask the guard, Sam, if I can have
a door. He said he would shoot me
somewhere unmentionable.
But I assure you, I never
knew his cousin.

Wordless, I sit at the desk
they call mine and crash
to the floor seven times.
This is nothing
like on television, the smells
make me nauseous. There are no
windows, never mind doors!

Sam doesn't believe a word I say —
but it's true: rats run the entire facility.
We hardly give them enough credit.
No one looks me in the eye
and everywhere I look: pinstripe kilts
run loose like germs.

My arms rattle, this overdose
is all placebo. I still get hard
when I remember
hyperventilation. Did they think
they were underwater?

Believe me, I signed up
for every program
that would take me.
I have a busy schedule,
I am sincere. No time for you.

Sincerely. Time's up.

Chest Out, Stomach In

"…the surgeons have to have someone to practise on."

Ragged nails, calluses from rope. My right hand
holds a pencil; my left pulls the paper.
The pencil checks the box next to the name
I like best — hold still. They let me do this now,
all of us whose heads reach the line
on the clown's outstretched palm.

The attendants frown at my calluses,
don't return my crooked smile.
I don't know what they do
with my slip of folded paper
after I slide it into the box
and walk out of the basement.

I wear a green uniform most days,
but not today. I don't want to confuse
the others in line, waiting for pencils.
I can fire a gun with either hand.
They let us do this now, those
who can run fast enough.

I don't know what they did
with the report I filed,
the one I wrote with my right hand
after I walked off the base.
I never painted my nails, I had calluses,
I asked for nothing, not that.
Not that.

Besides tuition, another benefit
is free cosmetic surgery. This was not folded
into the brochure—they let me know
after my nose was in splinters.
I am in line for breast augmentation too,
though it will be harder to run.

The Beauty Killer
Poems

Gaona, a former stripper, began working as plastic surgeon in 1998, and through word of mouth she soon became the rage of Guadalajara. . . . Women travelled from as far away as California and Texas to see "la doctora," who, patients say, prominently displayed a supposed licence on her clinic wall.

— Alicia Calderon, "La doctora mutilated my soul"

La Doctora kills a chicken

A city without beauty,
sectioned by chicken wire,
razor wire. Herr Doktor,
La Doctora. Precision mapped
targets, ownership's
little scraps. Keep out.

All the men in jail or ravines.
Their reek of secrets. Slow rot
complacency of dirt.
We are still

here. Mama, lost
in a cardboard Mary
shrine, ringed by
small fires, incense smothering
the new baby brother. She slurs
prayers for the gashes
in her family. Memory full
of faith — vanishes.

Can't hear us rumbling
hungry children.
I drip milk into the squalling
boy. Wet tongue
bubbling up, a raw thing —
alive. Chicken blood

lines my fingernails, wing tip
veils blur my eyes.
It is the first time
I killed one, just me.
The crunch and squelch
of skull and brain. Feathers
cling to my rock
like guilt, like shame.

Mama is eating the bible
again. Hates the living, wants
only truth. I eat pages
of *Vogue*. Want to grow
tits, and fashion —

escape this rictus, this
valley. Papa Cruz next door
winks a deal. Shakes my hand,
dead lizard fists.
He'll pluck it for us,
one night only —
if I sit with him,
in his lap awhile.

That night I throw
the feet at Mama.
Kicking over walls.
Tangles shrill in her
hair. Three nights
clamped over
us, like mouths.

La Doctora surveys her clientele

Shame stretched,
they come to me.
Bloated, canvas of hurt, I am
repulsed. Curl into myself
like a yard snake.

The women shuffle
and heave at my door
in track-suit folds.
Even their dreams sweat. They flinch

at the slightest touch, bruise
so easily. That's why
they're here.

Like American prom queens
scheming their own
funerals. A tear in every eye.
Heavy as ripe fruit, determined
to drop. The sun, a siege
in their kitchens,

screeches morning. The dishes
march toward them in rows.
Firing squad precision.

The poorest plead
the currency
of desperation.
When husband
turns at night
to thin daughter.

For a price, I can
fix this. Still,
I don't want to touch them.
This weakness, a contagion,
can jump like fleas,
from their arms to mine.
The blood we all want.

To smile and not crack
like clay without rain.
I whisper, love will fall
from above.

Dishes will not break,
and husbands will sleep
in their own beds.

Today their front lawns
try to swallow them whole.
Thirsty yards buckle and lurch.
They hurtle down sidewalks,
a wobbling stiletto panic.

I offer the end of a rope.
A doorway. A promise.
That heads will turn —
and fall into their laps.

La Doctora goes to church

A town stifled
into rows. Hats perched
on heads like heads
on stakes. Bibles

slump, then turn
into fans. The air,
impure with heat.

Mama drags me,
shining. End
of her arm. A bright
new handbag.

Pressed smooth,
scrubbed pink as meat
we can't afford. Sock

with only one hole,
my shoe's secret
captive.

Sunday ruffles choke
these socks — Mama found them
crowning the garbage bin

in a house she cleans.
Scrubs toilets every day
and we have none.

Ungodly to shit
in the house. She crosses
herself, lips clamped, humming
to the outhouse.

Saints blaze
above us. Hearts,
radiant and open,

blood-perfect,
but I know
Mama's heart pulses

no Jesus-glow.
Cold fingers pinch
my arm: *keep quiet.*

Sweat-heavy dress
steals the air
from my chest —

the walls twist
around me and
in pours red.

Outside, my friends slip
like lizards
into the river.

Hymn books flap open,
a flock of birds
with broken wings.

Mama stands to sing,
bloated canary. I seethe,
slither to the floor.
Pull my legs to the aisle.

The shoes kick
away first. The socks,
unrepentant, clump
behind. Clicks and whispers
from the pews.

I grow fat
with fury, the buttons
on my dress fly off

like popcorn, skip
loud as coins spilled
from collection plates.

The dress collapses,
damp and lifeless
in the aisle —

my unmoving
shadow. I run.
Fall without sound
into the river.

The sun ducks
behind the next town.
Mama slaps my face
red as hers. Dirty girl,

head full of filth. Locks me
in the outhouse to pray —
forgive me, father —
until morning.

A trapped bird
tries to fly
through sky cracks.
Lands a ruin
of feathers at my feet.
A warm glow

pours from his chest.
I reach in, cup
my hands.
His heart —
alight and pure.

La Doctora pours a drink

Sulking, I unlock a cabinet, not full
of silicone. Dash in a wave of tequila.
Melted gold, I call it —
God-piss, says Pedro.

The nights slide into a darker cool,
the men grow louder,
rumbling over streets,
spitting and pinching when you're not looking —

even worse when you are. I curl my fingers
tight around the mug, knuckles snap
like cap guns, wired with veins more purple
than I remember, regal and mechanized.

I line my eyes with kohl.
This is my Egypt, I command
what goes into and what comes out of
these kneeling bodies.

The dunes roll and I beckon.
Pyramids rise in my image.
The sign heralds "Beauty Clinic"
— I am the richest unmarried woman in Guadalajara.

"More?" Pedro grunts, sloshing the tin pot.
I stroke the lions on either side of me.
Pedro is brave, he takes the cup, dodges the snakes,
coiled and jewelled, writhing around my arms.

La Doctora makes a friend

The chorus line of hope and envy
darts its eyes, cranes its neck
around the block.

I don't advertise. All tongue,
women talk, compete. Today
I pluck a blonde from the queue.

Spine haughty and straight —
I read postures like auras, hers erect
like the middle finger she gives

to a passing car, the honking goose
leaking oil and rusting,
guided by a lead foot and a leer.

Her face unchanged, nose tipped up —
I wonder whose it is. I don't do noses
yet. The splinter of cartilage

I've heard only in bars, never my office.
Certain she'll be chronic, a regular,
I toss Pedro a coin, sneak her through the back.

New in town, she dodges questions,
a black car circles the clinic, humming
an obvious tune. No cigars, no rust flaking

like factory workers' skin, he's not cruising
for bikini bargains — a glance out back
tells Pedro there's a badge deep in that jacket pocket.

Her man must be small change, a cop
so green, so obvious, one of them will be cold
by dinnertime. I offer her a half-dozen services,

she says no to nothing. She doesn't want to be
recognized. Vanity swallows logic
like the snake's tail. A flawed woman

is invisible, but that will not be her.
She can afford beauty, slaps down cash.
Soon I will buy an air conditioner.

Screens sift the gossip of circling buzzards,
something near must be bleeding.
I trace her cheek and tug,

dotting her future in black marker.
I will fill this up, round and smooth.
She almost smiles. Out back, a car door

opens, soft as cracking an egg.

La Doctora interns in facial transplants

A laboratory in Louisville, rows of fluorescent lights
buzzing like saws. In Vancouver, a building
burns, from the seventh floor.

Missing hands want to be replaced,
and have. Failed livers
are filled with resentment.

Accidents crouch under eighteen-wheelers.
Drivers shredded, from shoulders down.
The highways are littered with donors.

Worse than a storm-hunter, I stalk fatalities
of all kinds, coax science and philanthropy
from mourning — so beauty stays intact.

The woman on the Granville Street balcony
could have climbed down, unscathed. Her six year old
clung to the kitchen floor, terrified.

She carried him down seven flights.
Eighty per cent of her skin: gone.
Eight years later, I mail her the package.

Is she still single? Send her the Julia Roberts prototype.
They all keep their own bone structure,
every one is different, don't worry about that!

Today I see my drug dealer ex-boyfriend
wearing that cheap green suit, minus bullet holes.
He buys King crab in Chinatown.

I run toward him — he's forgotten
his deathly allergy to shellfish.

Fully Autonomous
Planets

. . . listen: there's a hell
of a good universe next door;let's go

— e.e. cummings

The Informant

Clinking glasses with the best of them —
it is up to the informant
to ferret out fault, accountability;
we are all trafficking in blame.

I have some in my pocket,
cozy with lint, a strip club
matchbook and an American nickel.
Where did that come from?
I bet it is a bug, I bet
my fillings are bar-coded,
no wonder I chatter —
I mean, no wonder my teeth.

This bunker is cold
and, intermittently, it rumbles.
Our hosts are nowhere.
I want another martini,
but first I will engrave
my initials on this wall.
I was here.

The Urban Planner

Shanghai is plummeting into itself.
The marshland it's perched on
a toreador — having been patient — now
waves a red square. Tickles the feet
of the subway. Thousands of cupolas lean
in, unable to resist a dare.

This is a truck stop, I order whatever
refuses to curdle when I look.
No trucks actually stop,
but that one just unfurled a coat
of gravel over the road, no doubt
the streetcars will complain.
No doubt the driver meant to turn
off Loretta Lynn.

I have seven blisters — this gravel
was lying from the outset.
I incarcerate my feet, or is that
my father? A waiter smashes
the stemware, hands me a spill-proof
mug. It lurches and the jury spurns
the streetcars, finds the ground
guilty of treason.

The Superintendent

My teeth are leaping from my head.
Roots tipped skyward, bone white,
dangle parachute threads.
Vein webs. Safety nets
dissolve in the fray.

Grace and mutiny, the plummet.
Swan dive, un-mine.
The incisors skip
along unfamiliar roads.
In tandem with glee.

I sigh, gurgle a little —
dole out gum-fuls of love.
The Superintendent of Fraud
is in the waiting room.
This is our honeymoon.

Our Oncology Suite.
Glowing numbers keep us company,
a green receiving line.
My jaws twitch. Grin, they say,
grin and bite down hard.

The Paratrooper

We land in silence. The first snowfall?
Everyone forgets how to drive.
We issue citations for apathy, banality
and lingering depression. My mailbox is full.

Our uniforms are white, like all uniforms now.
On every veranda we whisper, "Next is the Gobi again,
just as soon as we fix up this town."

Ammonia rushes the streets like a flood
and the gas mask vendors make another killing.
I trip over a pothole, tear my knee and stain
my brand new uniform.

The feral cats of dawn begin to beam.
They will claw at the sun and blink
their small headlights.

I taste the nearness of it —
morning's mint and a bloody lip. If they give me stitches,
I will be demoted, forced to guard
a desert full of babies. I'm terrified

they'll climb down
from those fence posts
and take a run at me.

The New Mayor

The town is a banquet of winking adulterers,
several municipal cover-ups and a back alley
stabbing blamed on the suicide note.

The shoreline has grown wooden posts
that flower into sturdy red signs: "Off Limits."
Rows of children sob as their beach balls hiss.
Mismanagement desiccates the turkey farm,
the hockey team, the pickle factory.

The bars run out of glasses, even on Tuesdays.
The mayor sells his cottage to an aging Ohio couple
and disappears. The new mayor steps off the bus, dusts
turkey feathers from his lapels and shouts,

"This town needs some incentive to get back on its feet:
high-octane fuel injection, some Go pills,
a new felt hat!" No one remembers voting for him,
but we shake his hand, snap his picture and wave
at his lurching float in the Turkey Festival parade.

A rusty Mac revs its engine. We heave
from our lawn chairs; he could be hauling
just about anything into town.

The Contractor

The porcelain shatters.
A geyser, unsupervised, determined.
Leaping into air, celebratory, free — getting intimate
with carpets, floorboards, ceilings, walls. All without consent.

The water swims under doors, rushes down
the highway to find you in town, sipping coffee.
It licks your toes, as if to say, "Come with me,
you'll love what we've done with the place."

At home you find no leprechaun
sitting gleeful atop the fountain,
no pot of gold, not even a rainbow
over the lakes in every room.

Just a sub-par contractor and reams of insurance claims,
strips of wallpaper torn from the kitchen.
The oven still works though, and all that crying,
that swearing, makes you hungry.

I'm too busy to take a turn at the mop
and I'm sorry the kitten drowned —
but luck won't always bite into a rotten apple.
At least you'll get a new kitchen, some dry potatoes.

The Box Office Manager

Tickets to the benediction are for sale,
but the recording drones "Sold out."
The recording used to be
my next door neighbour —
I hear it's a good job,
if you don't mind union dues.

The first five rows are best,
proximity is status, ego dead centre,
but here I am, locked outside.

A pigeon flits past my head,
urges me to a better show —
no tickets, no service charges,
no intermission and sure
to change my life.

First I must uncurl my fingers
from the box office manager's neck.
A significant challenge,
yaps the sudden memo
that unfolds from his mouth.

My hands say they are happy there —
productivity is up.
The manager seems glad
for the break from faking reports.

"Fine," I say, "You're coming too."
The pigeon tilts and nods,
restless to tell me the truth:
he isn't really a pigeon,
but an unusually chatty cruise missile.

"Hold the depleted uranium,"
I say, "I'm with you all the way.
You and me and this slumping
hanger-on, take us to your off-off Broadway."
No marquee, just steel doors
swung open. My missile whispers,
"The ushers are invisible."

Three plush seats dust themselves off,
front row. I readjust the box office manager's
silk tie. The curtain flies up,
a guillotine in reverse.

A red spotlight singes
my next door neighbour centre stage:
he *is* a pigeon. He blinks and says
nothing, still a recording.

Standing room only and no rustling
candy wrappers. "Candy is extinct,"
blinks the pigeon — I know
Morse code. *What a performance*
I think, *I had no idea my neighbour
had such talent.* Now we're lining up

at his feet — he's passing something out.
I cup my hands, ready
for a blessing. It's about time.
It is small and colder than I expect,
but fits in the pocket over my heart.

I skip through the lobby,
things will get better now —
the pigeon says there is enough
depleted uranium for everyone.
An open-ended run.

The Orthodontist

He lurches awake in the suburbs,
shivering against the stubborn dark
fighting a losing battle with dawn.

The clock's uncertainty, the overlap —
night pulls its hood over its head
and rushes — whether at you, or past you,
is never clear. Dreams overflow

his eyes. He was a tightrope
walker, perfect straightness
languid before him, all
he had to do, for once, was follow.

Below, small mounds of enamel
smouldered. He was angry
at the lifetime of mutinous jaws —
sore, humiliated children.

The orthodontist put one foot
in front of the other — an expert
in evenness. Finally, his chance to stretch
to his full height, to straighten up.

The Pilot

The sky purples and hisses,
spits down its thousand teeth.
Hailstones the size of apples
aim for windshields, bay
windows, the heads of stray dogs.

I don't know what control means
this week. Variables won't negotiate
with boundaries; vines don't respect
fences. I went to bed early.
Naturally, there was another plane crash.

I once knew a reasonably successful
artist. Hard work has a thousand
teeth, but we used to be orthodontists.
Really — that's why we still speak.
His seat was H-15. When you have
long legs, you know to request the aisle.

The plummet was planned
and perpendicular to the yard —
it's not easy to accelerate
at ninety degrees! The nose
pierced through first, clean out
the other side of the planet.

I opened my eyes to where
his plane should have broke ground.
There was nothing left but an inverse
mirage: the nose intact, gleaming erect —
a silver carrot, growing into the sky.

The Kleptomaniac

Bright blue eye shadow, refills
for a glue gun, a bag of nuts
to which she is allergic. A co-operative
waistband, a slip folded up,
a few safety pins — tricks pilfered
from young adult novels.

An angry father, a lingering
reluctance to leave home, a sudden
inability to inhale. Silent hands that scrape,
encircle hips. Snags in nylon bunched
waist-high. A sense of falling without
a net — a joke flung over the head.

The clouds opening, all the missing
houses tumbling, a Houdini-like trinket
euphoria. A will scrawled longhand,
stashed under the mattress. A laundry basket
spilling immaculate glut — a hyena's laugh,
a man with a gun, another half-whispered riddle.

The Fisherman

This table sags under heaps of lobster, shrimp, snapper.
Edging toward us, left of sunburns, is the ocean —
determined to snatch back its fish.

On this island, yelling bounces off the water: "Yo, Chinaman!"
from the taxi driver to the East Indian giving directions.
I am from Canada, land of seatbelts and lifejackets.

This beachside seafood lunch is the best we've had
and we say so, raising our voices over a woman
wailing, inhuman, on shore. We ask for more drinks

and an explanation. A local
tells us that her son didn't come back up
from this morning's lobster dive.

The Carnie

I did not wish for summer;
nonetheless, it forces its blonde
diatribe upon me, a pox of umbrellas,
squealing children in queues and Over
Under weight games.

I step up to the scaffold, the man with the megaphone
will guess the eating disorder of the day.
Everyone wins. The clouds split open,
the sun's monologue begins.

The carnie does not foretell the future
by examining the entrails of the sacrificed,
nor will he chart the patterns of lightning
as it cracks the day during funerals.

Before stepping up, I read the rules.
We are to learn only from the day before.
For example, he raised the shovel
high above his head, enraged by questions —

caught the answer on the tip of the blade,
and soon joined her underground.
I vow to suggest a few new rules
for the day after tomorrow.

The Surgeon General

Hair gushes from her head, flaming
persimmons at her temples, a tall stride
and secrets you cannot keep time with.

You're right about justice, how it packed up
and fled town in the fall of last year,
its head rattling and winding
like a bobbin, too many holes.

The doctor choked by his own
stethoscope, the twins still laughing,
"Mom, Mom, look, he's so good,
so real!" And her calm smile, how it slid
down her face into a hot pool of panic.

Shot twice in her own apartment,
toppled jars of estrogen, crushed persimmons,
not even a nail broken, not even
finished the rest of her surgeries.
A cold, defaced Barbie.

The Skater

The wind lowers its cracked hand,
swipes sap from the trees — they shiver
a new hue. High Park valleys ripple
red, orange, gold sinews. October's muscle.

Summer's drowned in a lake of flattened
beach balls. I can breathe.
Fall crackles into focus,
the rinks spread their doors wide.

I join adults in borrowed helmets,
new bruises and kids' skates. The ice
is bone-smooth, a glowing glacier.

I grind into it, calligraphic —
etching portents — a flourish
of snow howls in chorus.

The Campaign Manager

He hurls a fistful of commas
over his head and they etch
a sporadic though deadly
litany against the ozone.

They had been lined up,
chattering and bouncing
at the voting booths,
even though all these new machines
are defective, x turning
into y — and so on.

Meanwhile, the parishioners
don't respond, stubborn particles
that they are. It is more lecture
than litany anyway. Or assault,
those tails no longer cute,
the curls curling to barbs. Or,
if this is a prison, their inky
little asses are shanks.

The Vice-President

My diet scuttles by, I am sure
he stole my stereo. Little bastard
is bloated with greed, and it is best
not to mention the mange
that has gnawed away
a good half of his head.

Too bad it wasn't
the part that connives
with the vice president,
sits on the board
of his multinational.

The same one who bought
my grandmother's house,
including the orchard
where I climb
trees and build fully
autonomous planets.

My diet and I aren't really
getting along,
he pays no rent
and takes up most of the space.

The vice president ripped
my grandma off, that house —
not to mention the orchard —
was worth much more,

but the other half of my diet's head
made up some lies about mould and rot —
a cache of weapons stashed
beneath the compost heap.

I miss my grandma,
not to mention the planets.

The Miner

Spirograph pieces rattle,
nudge the box open.
Decide to run their own show,
pens unravelling designs
wound tight in tiny springs.

A baby sleeps, exhausted
by its howls. The cradle
swings itself
after a fight.

A half-empty drink
reflects a storm
about to split open.

A miner finds an unfinished
equation etched in granite.
He claws the air,
finds no resistance.

Something terminal, viral,
opens the doors of every home,
swarms in like fruit flies,
appears on no guest list.

The spirals are taped to every wall,
momentum found without hills,
tumbling turned reckless
and addictive.

The Offshore Banker

A fair trade, glasses are raised,
your pile of paper for mine.
This stands for that, and nothing

is ever cashed. An accusation of extortion,
a sparrow in the kitchen, a fork in the road.
An imminent sense of calamity, then somnambulism.

You run a brisk trade in agility.
Your shares in me will bankrupt us both.

All this longing, this skinflint love —
in numbered accounts, offshore.

A retreat to the suburbs,
an unsuccessful dermabrasion:

still drawn, convicted, to you.

The Real Estate Developer

The empty lot should have been a sign.
Omens are everywhere —
teeth nestled coyly in gravel, sometimes
my own. In that shrub, a hammer,
presumably rusted. Before that, a trivet,
snatched home. Domesticity
for mistresses.

A truck stop bar, dropped Kansas-style
from September's hurricane. Perched
at the edge of a slaughterhouse, steadfast
ramparts. The developers keep blood
deep in their pockets.

Cheap pints, a layer of cream like two knees on the chest.
Honesty without currency, all partition,
and keys in locks. I can see across the vacancy,
the savannah is waist high. My lungs

are bellicose. I will become
the rainy season, a tidal wave of shrapnel.

Notes on the Text

The epigraph, title and subject matter for "Chest Out, Stomach In" come from Karen Schaler's "Chest Out, Stomach In: All That You Can Be" (*The New Yorker*, July 26, 2004).

The Beauty Killer Poems were inspired by "La doctora mutilated my soul," an article by Alicia Calderon which appeared in the *Toronto Star* (October 13, 2002).

"La Doctora interns in facial transplants" was inspired by a CBC radio documentary ("The Current," October, 2004) about the ethics of face transplants.

Acknowledgements

A huge thank you goes out to the following for their support and encouragement during the writing of these poems: Sandra Alland, Andrea Blundell, Kevin Connolly, Bryan Muraki, Stuart Ross. Each of them fuelled this process in their own way, for which I am enormously grateful.

The following poems have previously appeared elsewhere, in an earlier incarnation:

A version of "Shred" first appeared in Thirteenth Tiger Press' chapbook "Night of the Prom" in 2002.

A version of "The Lifeboat" was first published in *100 Poets Against the War* (Salt Publishing, 2003).

Taddle Creek magazine published "La Doctora surveys her clientele" in its Summer 2004 issue.